MEMOIR OF
SUSIE KING TAYLOR

A
CIVIL WAR NURSE

by Pamela Dell

Content Adviser:
Brett Barker, PhD
Associate Professor of History
University of Wisconsin-Marathon County

CAPSTONE PRESS
a capstone imprint

Fact Finders are published by Capstone Press,
1710 Roe Crest Drive, North Mankato, Minnesota 56003
www.mycapstone.com

Library of Congress Cataloging-in-Publication Data
Names: Dell, Pamela, author.
Title: Memoir of Susie King Taylor : a Civil War nurse / by Pamela Dell.
Description: North Mankato, Minnesota : Capstone Press, [2017 | Series: Fact finders.
First-person histories | Includes bibliographical references and index. | Audience: Grades 4-6. |
Audience: Ages 10-12.
Identifiers: LCCN 2016038565| ISBN 9781515733546 (library binding) | ISBN 9781515733560
(paperback) | ISBN 9781515733584 (ebook : pdf)
Subjects: LCSH: Taylor, Susie King, 1848-1912—Juvenile literature. | African American nurses—
Biography—Juvenile literature. | Nurses—Southern States—Biography—Juvenile literature.
| United States—History—Civil War, 1861-1865—African Americans—Juvenile literature.
| United States. Army. Colored Infantry Regiment, 33rd (1864-1866)—Biography—Juvenile
literature. | United States Army—Nurses—Biography—Juvenile literature. | United States—
History—Civil War, 1861-1865—Women—Juvenile literature. | African American women—
Biography—Juvenile literature.
Classification: LCC E621.T3 D45 2016 | DDC 973.7/75092 [B]—dc23
LC record available at https://lccn.loc.gov/2016038565

Editorial Credits
Catherine Neitge, editor; Bobbie Nuytten and Catherine Neitge, designers; Svetlana Zhurkin,
media researcher; Kathy McColley, production specialist

Photo Credits
Alamy: Thomas R. Fletcher, 13; Courtesy Documenting the American South/UNC-Chapel Hill
Library, 12; Getty Images: Fotosearch, 11 (bottom); Library of Congress, cover (inset on the
left, right), 1, 5, 6, 7, 8, 9, 14, 15, 16, 17, 19, 22, 25, 27, 29; Newscom: Picture History, 21;
Shutterstock: Globe Turner, 11 (African continent), MaluStudio 11 (flag of Liberia), pavalena
(map of Liberia), Robert B. Miller, 20; design elements by Shutterstock

Source Notes
Page 4, line 18: Susie King Taylor. *Reminiscences of My Life in Camp with the 33d United States
Colored Troops Late 1st S.C. Volunteers.* Boston: By the author, 1902, p. 5.
Page 15, col. 1, line 4: Camp Saxton Site. South Carolina Department of Archives and History.
19 Sept. 2016. www.nationalregister.sc.gov/beaufort/S10817707057/
Page 15, col. 2, line 3: *Official Records of the Union and Confederate Armies.*
Washington, D.C.: Government Printing Office, 1885, p. 190.
Page 17, sidebar, line 13: Thomas Wentworth Higginson. *Army Life in a Black Regiment.*
Boston and New York: Houghton Mifflin Company, 1900, p. 359.

Editor's Note
This book contains only portions of Susie King Taylor's memoir, *Reminiscences of My Life in
Camp with the 33d United States Colored Troops Late 1st S.C. Volunteers.* It was published in 1902
and is available online at the Library of Congress: http://lcweb2.loc.gov/service/gdc/scd0001/200
8/20081001004re/20081001004re.pdf

Printed and bound in the United States of America.
10029S17

TABLE OF CONTENTS

A Young Black Nurse in a Military Camp

Susie Baker was born a slave on August 6, 1848, the eldest of nine children. Her family was enslaved on Georgia's Isle of Wight, one of the Sea Islands that lie along the coast of South Carolina and Georgia. The islands' slaves worked on plantations and had little hope of ever gaining their freedom. That changed when the Civil War started in 1861.

The southern states had declared themselves a new nation called the Confederate States of America. They were fighting against the northern states, called the Union. The South did not want the federal government interfering in its individual states' decisions. This especially applied to the widespread practice of slavery. The northern states had long ago outlawed slavery and did not want it to spread.

But even before the war began, Susie had more good fortune than most. At 7 she was sent to Savannah, Georgia, to live with her grandmother. There, she learned to read and write in a secret school. "We went every day about nine o'clock," Susie wrote later, "with our books wrapped in paper to prevent the police or white persons from seeing them." It was against the law for enslaved people to learn to read or write.

The Sea Islands were home to some of the largest and wealthiest cotton plantations in the South. The black enslaved population on the islands outnumbered the whites 83 percent to 17 percent.

Less than a year after the Civil War began, Susie's life took a dramatic turn. Union troops drove the whites from the Sea Islands and freed the enslaved people there. From the islands' slaves the nation's first **regiment** of African-American soldiers was formed, called the 1st South Carolina Volunteers. The volunteers, who included escaped slaves from South Carolina and Florida, proved so brave in battle that President Abraham Lincoln and other northerners saw the value of creating more black regiments.

Susie King Taylor

Susie, just 14 when the regiment formed, became its **laundress**. She also married one of the volunteers, Sergeant Edward King. As a young wife, Susie King lived and traveled with the regiment as it moved from camp to camp. Because she was educated, she also taught the soldiers and served as a battlefield nurse.

In 1902 Susie published her memories of that historic time in her youth. *Reminiscences of My Life in Camp with the 33d United States Colored Troops Late 1st S.C. Volunteers* details Susie's exceptional experience. Few women, black or white, left such a detailed and interesting account of what it was like to live in a Civil War camp. For Susie it was a view of the fight for freedom seen up close.

regiment—large group of soldiers who fight together as a unit

laundress—woman who washes and irons clothes

5

THE Memoir OF Susie King Taylor
1862–1866

April 1, 1862—

...[A]bout the time the Union soldiers were firing on Fort Pulaski, I was sent out into the country to my mother. I remember what a roar and din the guns made. They jarred the earth for miles. The fort was at last taken by them [Union soldiers].

April 13, 1862—

[M]y uncle took his family of seven and myself to St. Catherine Island. We landed under the protection of the Union fleet.

Wherever possible, Susie's recollections of her Civil War experiences appear word for word as they were written. Because she wrote her book many years after the Civil War ended, the exact dates of some of her recollections may be slightly incorrect. Many have approximate dates or no dates at all. Because Susie's memoir appears in its original form, you may find a few uncommon expressions. To make the meanings of these words more clear, explanations within a set of brackets follow. Also, in some places, words have been removed from the memoir entries. In these cases, you will notice three dots in a row, called ellipses. They show that words or sentences are missing from the text.

Fort Pulaski suffered battle scars during the long siege by Union forces.

Fort Pulaski sat on Georgia's Cockspur Island close to the mouth of the Savannah River. Having control of the fort was important to Union troops. From there they could prevent Confederate ships from entering or leaving Savannah, an important port city. The Union siege of the fort lasted 112 days and ended with a victorious battle on April 10 and 11.

siege—prolonged attack designed to surround a place and cut it off from supplies or help

Around April 27, 1862—

[A]bout thirty of us were taken aboard the gunboat P_____, to be transferred to St. Simons Island; and at last, to my unbounded joy, I saw the "Yankee." ...

Next morning we arrived at St. Simons. ... After I had been on St. Simons about three days, Commodore Goldsborough heard of me, and came to Gaston Bluff to see me. [He] wished me to take charge of a school for the children on the island. I told him I would gladly do so ... I had about forty children to teach, beside[s] a number of adults who came to me nights, all of them so eager to learn to read, to read above anything else.

St. Catherines Island and St. Simons Island, about 50 miles (80 kilometers) south of Savannah, are two of the Sea Islands that lie along the coast of Georgia and South Carolina.

The *Commodore McDonough* gunboat helped enforce a blockade in South Carolina waters.

Yankees

During the Civil War, southerners referred to people from the North as Yankees. Beginning in World War I and continuing today, people from other parts of the world call all Americans Yankees or Yanks. The term may have first been used by a British general during the Revolutionary War.

In her memoir, Susie wrote about Yankees: "I had been reading so much about the 'Yankees' I was very anxious to see them. The whites would tell their colored people not to go to the Yankees, for they would harness them to carts and make them pull the carts around, in place of horses. I asked grandmother, one day, if this was true. She replied, 'Certainly not!' that the white people did not want slaves to go over to the Yankees, and told them these things to frighten them."

blockade—military effort to keep goods from entering and leaving a region

Commodore Louis M. Goldsborough was a Union naval commander. He was one of the officers in charge of blockading the coast so supplies could not get to the South.

Early summer 1862—

About the first of June we were told that there was going to be a settlement of the war. Those who were on the Union side would remain free, and those in bondage were to work three days for their masters and three for themselves. It was a gloomy time for us all, and we were to be sent to Liberia. Chaplain French asked me would I rather go back to Savannah or go to Liberia. I told him the latter place by all means. We did not know when this would be, but we were prepared in case this settlement should be reached. However, the Confederates would not agree to the arrangement, or else it was one of the many rumors flying about at the time, as we heard nothing further of the matter. …

One Sunday, two men … were chased by some rebels … but the latter were unable to catch them. When they reached the Beach and told this, all the men on the place, about ninety, armed themselves, and next day (Monday) … **skirmished** the island for the "rebs." In a short while they discovered them in the woods, hidden behind a large log, among the thick underbrush.

skirmish—small fight

Liberia was formed in 1822 as a western African homeland for freed U.S. slaves. It became an independent country in 1847. About 15,000 African-Americans settled there on land purchased by the American Colonization Society. But any large-scale movement like the one Taylor described was just a rumor circulating among southern blacks. They were afraid they would not be allowed to be free and remain in the United States.

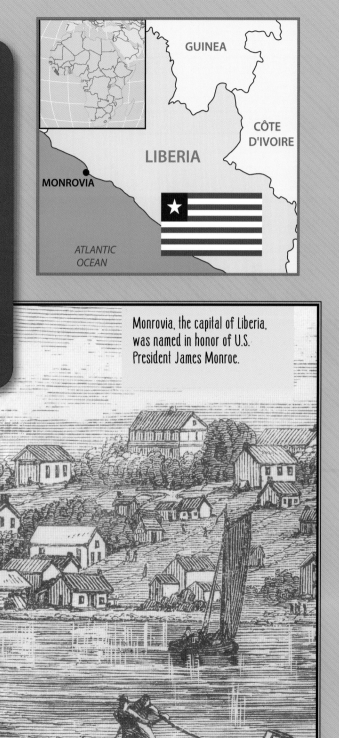

GUINEA

CÔTE D'IVOIRE

LIBERIA

MONROVIA

ATLANTIC OCEAN

Monrovia, the capital of Liberia, was named in honor of U.S. President James Monroe.

11

Late August 1862—

Captain C.T. Trowbridge ... came to St. Simons Island from Hilton Head, by order of General Hunter, to get all the men possible to finish filling his regiment which he had organized in March, 1862. He had heard of the skirmish on this island, and was very much pleased at the bravery shown by these men. He found me at Gaston Bluff teaching my little school, and was much interested in it. When I knew him better I found him to be a thorough gentleman and a staunch friend to my race.

C.T. Trowbridge

Captain Charles Tyler Trowbridge was a white officer who led the 1st South Carolina Volunteers. Susie referred to him as "jolly and pleasing with all" and wrote that no officer in the army was more beloved than he. All regiments of black soldiers in the Union army were commanded by white officers.

The 1st South Carolina Volunteers was formed in August 1862. Captain Trowbridge brought one of its companies to St. Simons Island. Their aim was to flush out any remaining Confederates and keep the island in the hands of the Union. But a surprise awaited Trowbridge and his soldiers when they arrived. The island's black inhabitants had banded together and, in the skirmish, had already driven off the rebels themselves.

Freedom!

General David Hunter, commander of the Union's Department of the South, was strongly anti-slavery. In May 1862 he issued an order freeing the slaves in Georgia, South Carolina, and Florida. His order was quickly overturned by President Lincoln, who worried about its political effects. Lincoln thought that politicians, not generals, should make such an important decision. Lincoln's Emancipation Proclamation, which freed enslaved people in the Confederacy, took effect about six months later.

October 1862—

... [T]he order was received to evacuate, and so we boarded the *Ben-De-Ford*, a transport for Beaufort, S.C. When we arrived in Beaufort, Captain Trowbridge and the men he had enlisted went to camp at Old Fort, which they named "Camp Saxton." I was enrolled as laundress.

The first suits worn by the boys were red coats and pants, which they disliked very much, for, they said, "The rebels see us, miles away."

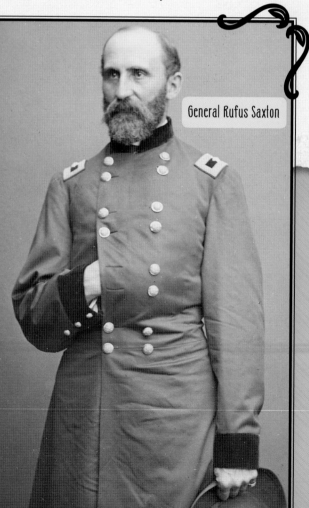

General Rufus Saxton

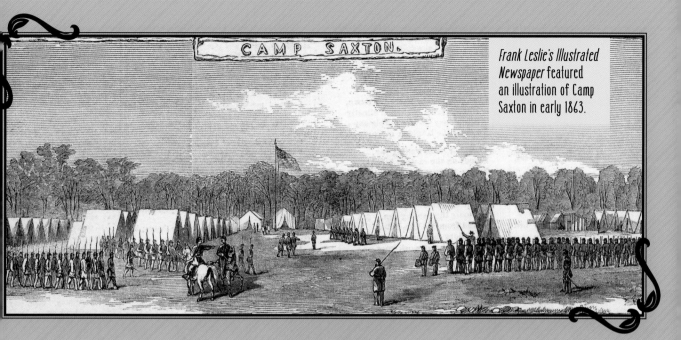

CAMP SAXTON.

Frank Leslie's Illustrated Newspaper featured an illustration of Camp Saxton in early 1863.

Camp Saxton

Camp Saxton, located in Beaufort County, South Carolina, was named for General Rufus Saxton. On August 22, 1862, Saxton had been authorized to "arm, equip, and receive into the service of the United States" up to 5,000 "volunteers of African descent." The 1st South Carolina Volunteers occupied the camp from early November 1862 through late January 1863.

General Saxton considered the plan to include black men in the Union Army a great success. He wrote to the U.S. Secretary of War, "... the negroes fought with a coolness and bravery that would have done credit to veteran soldiers. There was no excitement, no flinching, no attempt at cruelty when successful."

Tuesday, January 1, 1863—

...[W]e held services for the purpose of listening to the reading of President Lincoln's <u>proclamation</u>. ... It was a glorious day for us all, and we enjoyed every minute of it, and as a fitting close and the crowning event of this occasion we had a grand barbecue. A number of oxen were roasted whole, and we had a fine feast. Although not served as tastily or correctly as it would have been at home, yet it was enjoyed with keen appetites and relish. The soldiers had a good time. They sang or shouted "Hurrah!" all through the camp, and seemed overflowing with fun and frolic until **taps** were sounded, when many, no doubt, dreamt of this memorable day.

President Lincoln's Emancipation Proclamation freed the 3.5 million enslaved people in the areas of the South controlled by the Confederates. The remaining slaves, about 500,000 in border states, became free later. Slavery ended everywhere in the United States when the 13th Amendment was ratified in December 1865.

taps—the last bugle call blown at night as a signal that lights are to be put out; also often played at military funerals

expedition—journey made for a specific purpose

ABRAHAM LINCOLN

Emancipation Proclamation

January 23, 1863—

The regiment made an **expedition** ... up St. Mary's River, capturing a number of stores [supplies] for the government; then on to Fernandina, Florida. They were gone ten or twelve days, at the end of which time they returned to camp.

Thomas Wentworth Higginson

The purpose of the expeditions up the St. Mary's River and to Florida was to take all the food and supplies the regiment could get and to destroy what they could not take. Another aim was to bring to the Union side any enslaved people they came across. The expeditions were the 1st South Carolina Volunteers' first missions under the command of Colonel Thomas Wentworth Higginson. The lifelong foe of slavery led the regiment from November 1862 through October 1864.

After the war Higginson published *Army Life in a Black Regiment*, about his experiences with the 1st South Carolina Volunteers. "Till the blacks were armed," he wrote, "there was no guarantee of their freedom. It was their demeanor [behavior] under arms that shamed the nation into recognizing them as men."

March 10, 1863—

We were ordered to Jacksonville, Florida. Leaving Camp Saxton between four and five o'clock, we arrived at Jacksonville about eight o'clock next morning, accompanied by three or four gunboats. When the rebels saw these boats, they ran out of the city, leaving the women behind, and we found out afterwards that they thought we had a much larger fleet than we really had.

Our regiment was kept out of sight until we made fast at the wharf where it landed, and while the gunboats were **shelling** up the river and as far inland as possible, the regiment landed and marched up the street, where they spied the rebels who had fled from the city. They were hiding behind a house about a mile or so away, their faces blackened to disguise themselves as negroes, and our boys, as they advanced toward them, halted a second, saying, "They are black men! Let them come to us, or we will make them know who we are."

With this, the firing was opened and several of our men were wounded and killed. The rebels had a number wounded and killed. It was through this way the discovery was made that they were white men. Our men drove them some distance in retreat and then threw out their **pickets.**

shelling—heavy firing with cannons

pickets—soldiers posted on guard ahead of the main force

Union soldiers stood atop a signal tower in Jacksonville. The tower was more than 100 feet (30 meters) tall.

March 12, 1863—

On the third day, Edward Herron, who was a fine gunner on the steamer *John Adams* came on shore, bringing a small cannon, which the men pulled along for more than five miles. This cannon was the only piece for shelling. On coming upon the enemy, all secured their places, and they had a lively fight, which lasted several hours, and our boys were nearly captured by the Confederates; but the Union boys carried out all their plans that day, and succeeded in driving the enemy back. After this skirmish, every afternoon between four and five o'clock the Confederate General Finegan would send a flag of truce to Colonel Higginson …

Early April 1863—

We arrived at Seabrooke [near Beaufort] at about four o'clock, where our tents were pitched and the men put on duty. We were here a few weeks, when Company E was ordered to Barnwell plantation for picket duty.

Some mornings I would go along the picket line, and I could see the rebels on the opposite side of the river. Sometimes as they were changing pickets they would call over to our men and ask for something to eat, or for tobacco, and our men would tell them to come over. Sometimes one or two would desert to us, saying, they "had no negroes to fight for." [They were not slave owners.] Others would shoot across at our picket, but as the river was so wide there was never any damage done, and the Confederates never attempted to shell us while we were there.

I learned to handle a musket very well while in the regiment, and could shoot straight and often hit the target. I assisted in cleaning the guns and used to fire them off, to see if the cartridges were dry, before cleaning and reloading, each day. I thought this great fun. I was also able to take a gun all apart, and put it together again.

battery—position on a battlefield where cannons are located

A four-gun Confederate battery along the Mississippi River

April 1863—

One night, Companies K and E, on their way to Pocotaligo to destroy a **battery** that was situated down the river, captured several prisoners. The rebels nearly captured Sergeant King, [Susie's husband] who, as he sprang and caught a "reb," fell over an embankment. In falling he did not release his hold on his prisoner. Although his hip was severely injured, he held fast until some of his comrades came to his aid and pulled them up. These expeditions were very dangerous. Sometimes the men had to go five or ten miles during the night over on the rebel side and capture or destroy whatever they could find.

In addition to his rifle and bayonet, a Union soldier carried a bedroll, canteen, and haversack.

June 1864—

    Finally orders were received for the boys to prepare to take Fort Gregg, each man to take 150 rounds of **cartridges**, canteens of water, **hardtack**, and salt beef. This order was sent three days prior to starting, to allow them to be in readiness. I helped as many as I could to pack haversacks [canvas backpacks] and cartridge boxes.

July 2, 1864—

About four o'clock, July 2, the charge was made. The firing could be plainly heard in camp. I hastened down to the landing and remained there until eight o'clock that morning. When the wounded arrived, or rather began to arrive, the first one brought in was Samuel Anderson of our company. He was badly wounded. Then others of our boys, some with their legs off, arm gone, foot off, and wounds of all kinds imaginable. They had to wade through creeks and marshes, as they were discovered by the enemy and shelled very badly. A number of the men were lost, some got fastened in the mud and had to cut off the legs of their pants, to free themselves. The 103d New York suffered the most, as their men were very badly wounded.

My work now began. I gave my assistance to try to alleviate [ease] their sufferings. I asked the doctor at the hospital what I could get for them to eat. They wanted soup, but that I could not get; but I had a few cans of condensed milk and some turtle eggs, so I thought I would try to make some custard. I had doubts as to my success … [but] the result was a very delicious custard. This I carried to the men, who enjoyed it very much. My services were given at all times for the comfort of these men. I was on hand to assist whenever needed. I was enrolled as company laundress, but I did very little of it, because I was always busy doing other things through camp, and was employed all the time doing something for the officers and comrades.

cartridge—roll of thin paper which held a small amount of gunpowder in the bottom and a ball or bullet in the top

hardtack—hard, saltless biscuit used as food rations for armies

February 1865—

[T]he remainder of the regiment were ordered to Charleston, as there were signs of the rebels evacuating [leaving] that city. Leaving Cole Island, we arrived in Charleston between nine and ten o'clock in the morning, and found the "rebs" had set fire to the city and fled, leaving women and children behind to suffer and perish in the flames. The fire had been burning fiercely for a day and night. When we landed, under a flag of **truce**, our regiment went to work assisting the citizens in subduing the flames. It was a terrible scene.

For three or four days the men fought the fire, saving the property and effects of the people, yet these white men and women could not tolerate our black Union soldiers, for many of them had formerly been their slaves; and although these brave men risked life and limb to assist them in their distress, men and even women would sneer and molest [harass] them whenever they met them.

… I assisted in caring for the sick and injured comrades.

The Confederacy had been successful in defending the all-important city, Charleston, South Carolina, throughout the war. But in February 1865, southern troops gave up their defense and fled. Union troops took control of the burning and all but destroyed city. Citizens left behind faced disease, hunger, and homelessness. Other major southern cities—including Columbia, South Carolina, Atlanta, Georgia, and Richmond, Virginia—also experienced destruction from fire.

truce—temporary agreement to stop fighting

bushwhacker—fighter who lived in the woods and was not a member of the Confederate army

court-martial—military trial

Mid-April 1865—

The regiment remained in Augusta for thirty days, when it was ordered to Hamburg, S.C., and then on to Charleston. It was while on their march through the country, to the latter city, that they came in contact with the **bushwhackers** (as the rebels were called), who hid in the bushes and would shoot the Union boys every chance they got. Other times they would conceal themselves in the [railroad] cars used to transfer our soldiers, and when our boys, worn out and tired, would fall asleep, these men would come out from their hiding places and cut their throats.

Several of our men were killed in this way, but it could not be found out who was committing these murders until one night one of the rebels was caught in the act, trying to cut the throat of a sleeping soldier. He was put under guard, **court-martialed**, and shot at Wall Hollow.

Charleston, South Carolina, was one of many cities ruined during the Civil War.

February 9, 1866—

The following "General Orders" were received and the regiment mustered out [discharged from service].

General Order, No. 1.

Comrades: The hour is at hand when we must separate forever, and nothing can take from us the pride we feel, when we look upon the history of the "First South Carolina Volunteers," the first black regiment that ever bore arms in defense of freedom on the continent of America.

About 180,000 African-Americans fought for the Union army in the Civil War. Another 20,000 served in the Union navy.

On the 9th day of May, 1862, at which time there were nearly four millions of your race in bondage, sanctioned by the laws of the land and protected by our flag, ... you came forth to do battle for your country and kindred.

For long and weary months, without pay or even the privilege of being recognized as soldiers, you labored on ... And from that little band of hopeful, trusting, and brave men who gathered at Camp Saxton, on Port Royal Island, in the fall of '62, amidst the terrible prejudices that surrounded us, has grown an army of <u>140,000 black soldiers</u>, whose valor and heroism has won for your race a name which will live as long as the undying pages of history shall endure; and by whose efforts, united with those of the white man, armed rebellion has been conquered, the millions of bondsmen have been emancipated, and the fundamental law of the land has been so altered as to remove forever the possibility of human slavery being established within the borders of redeemed America. ... [A]nd as the result of your fidelity [faithfulness] and obedience you have won your freedom, and oh, how great the reward! ...

**By order of Lt. Colonel C.T. Trowbridge,
Commanding regiment**

Former enslaved men made up the ranks of the 1st South Carolina Volunteers.

In her memoir, Susie wrote—

They were delighted to go home, but oh! how they hated to part from their commanding chief, Colonel C.T. Trowbridge. He was the very first officer to take charge of black soldiers. We thought there was no one like him. ... All in the regiment knew him personally, and many were the jokes he used to tell them. I shall never forget his friendship and kindness toward me, from the first time I met him to the end of the war.

Life After the War

In camp as a teenage laundress, nurse, and teacher, Susie believed powerfully in the fight for her people's freedom. With the Union victory, she had high hopes for equality among the races. But she was disappointed.

Following the war, African-Americans experienced continued prejudice and racism in both the North and the South. As a grown woman Susie opened a school, and later moved to Boston, Massachusetts—all the while still longing for true racial equality.

Timeline

■ Dates in Susie King Taylor's life
■ Important dates in the Civil War

1861—April 12
The Civil War begins at Fort Sumter, South Carolina, when Confederate soldiers fire on the Union-held fort.

1848—August 6
Susie is born into slavery on the Isle of Wight, off the coast of Georgia.

1860—December 20
South Carolina secedes from the Union; 10 more states will eventually secede to form the Confederate States of America.

1845 — 1860

1862

Susie marries Edward King and joins the 1st South Carolina Volunteers as laundress, nurse, and teacher.

1912—October 6

Susie Baker King Taylor dies in Boston; she was 64.

1866

Susie and Edward return to Savannah, Georgia, where she starts a school for freed black children; Edward dies in an accident in September, shortly before the birth of their son.

1902

Susie publishes her book, *Reminiscences of My Life in Camp with the 33d United States Colored Troops Late 1st S.C. Volunteers.*

1863—January 1

President Abraham Lincoln's Emancipation Proclamation goes into effect.

1870s

Susie moves to Boston, Massachusetts, where she joins and then becomes president of the Women's Relief Corps, which gave assistance to soldiers and hospitals; she marries Russell L. Taylor in 1879.

1865—April 9

Confederate General Robert E. Lee surrenders to Union General Ulysses S. Grant in Virginia, ending the Civil War.

1898

Susie travels to Louisiana to be with her dying son.

1862   **1870**

Glossary

battery (BA-tuh-ree)—position on a battlefield where cannons are located

blockade (blok-ADE)—military effort to keep goods from entering and leaving a region

bushwhacker (bush-WACK-er)—fighter who lived in the woods and was not a member of the Confederate army

cartridge (KAHR-trij)—roll of thin paper that held a small amount of gunpowder in the bottom and a ball or bullet in the top

court-martial (KORT-mar-shuhl)—military trial

expedition (ek-spuh-DI-shuhn)—journey made for a specific purpose

hardtack (HARD-tak)—hard, saltless biscuit used as food rations for armies

laundress (LAWN-dress)—woman who washes and irons clothes

pickets (PIK-its)—soldiers posted on guard ahead of the main force

regiment (REJ-uh-muhnt)—large group of soldiers who fight together as a unit

shelling (SHEL-ing)—heavy firing with cannons

siege (SEEJ)—prolonged attack designed to surround a place and cut it off from supplies or help

skirmish (SKUR-mish)—small fight

taps (TAPS)—the last bugle call blown at night as a signal that lights are to be put out; also often played at military funerals

truce (TROOS)—temporary agreement to stop fighting

Read More

Baumann, Susan K. *Black Civil War Soldiers: The 54th Massachusetts Regiment.* New York: PowerKids Press, 2014.

Grayson, Robert. *The U.S. Civil War: Why They Fought.* North Mankato, Minn.: Compass Point Books, 2016.

Stanchak, John E. *Civil War.* New York: DK Publishing, 2015.

Critical Thinking Using the Common Core

1. On page 10 Susie writes about the possible early settlement of the war, and she is asked whether she would rather return to Savannah (as a slave) or go to Liberia (as a free person). She chooses Liberia. Research Liberia on the Internet and find out more. Why do you think Susie made this decision? (Integration of Knowledge and Ideas)

2. Susie lived in camp under dangerous conditions. Find some passages that show how she displayed her strength and courage. Do you think Susie's attitude and behavior would have been surprising to whites of her time who most likely had false ideas about blacks? Why or why not? (Craft and Structure)

3. On page 8 Susie talks about her "unbounded joy" at seeing "the Yankee." Why do you think she was so happy about this? What did "the Yankee" symbolize to her? (Craft and Structure)

4/17

Internet Sites

Use FactHound to find Internet sites related to this book. All of the sites on FactHound have been researched by our staff.

Here's all you do:

Visit *www.facthound.com*

Type in this code: 9781515733546

 **Super-cool stuff!** Check out projects, games and lots more at **www.capstonekids.com**

Index